The European Rediscovery of America

EXPLORATION
AND DISCOVERY

EXPLORATION
AND DISCOVERY

The European Rediscovery of America

How European explorers like Christopher Columbus, John Cabot, Amerigo Vespucci, Pedro Álvarez Cabral, and the Corte-Real brothers sailed to the continents they would call the New World

Kelly Wittmann

Mason Crest Publishers
Philadelphia

Mason Crest Publishers
370 Reed Road
Broomall PA 19008

Mason Crest Publishers' world wide web address is
www.masoncrest.com

First printing

1 3 5 7 9 8 6 4 2

Library of Congress Cataloging-in-Publication Data
on file at the Library of Congress

ISBN 1-59084-052-6

EXPLORATION AND DISCOVERY

Contents

A painting of Christopher Columbus gazing off the deck of his ship. Columbus made his 1492 voyage west across the Atlantic Ocean because he believed by that route he could reach the rich lands of the Far East—India, China, and Japan.

The Landing

"LAND!"

At two o'clock in the morning on October 11, 1492, a sailor named Rodrigo Bernajo cried out to his fellow seamen on the sailing ship *Pinta*. The leader of the voyage, Christopher Columbus, was roused from sleep and told the exciting news. After 10 weeks of sailing, he had been proven right—his ships had reached the Far East! For that is where Columbus thought he was. Not he, nor his men, nor anyone in Europe were aware that the continents of North and South America even existed.

For centuries, educated men had known that the world was round. That knowledge convinced Columbus that he could reach lands Columbus called the Indies—what we now know as China, Japan, and other countries of Asia—by sailing west across the Atlantic Ocean.

Prior to Columbus's voyage, the only way to get to the Indies was to travel east by land from Italy to Asia. Marco Polo had followed this route three centuries earlier. However, the road to the east was long and dangerous. Portugal was trying to find a sea route to Asia by sailing along the west coast of Africa, rounding the southern tip of the continent, then sailing east to India.

When Columbus set out in the opposite direction from the Portuguese, he could not have known that two huge continents populated by with millions of native people and many rich cultures stood between him and the Indies. As he gazed at the green coast in October 1492 he could not have known that it would become a new world for Europeans seeking freedom and liberty. Nor could he have forseen the the terrible price its native people would pay because of European exploration.

Columbus' brother, Bartholomew, was a mapmaker and sailor who worked with Columbus on many of his plans and voyages.

At daylight, Columbus sized up the situation. His three ships—the *Nina*, the *Pinta*, and the *Santa Maria*—appeared to be off the coast of an island that was about 12

This 19th-century illustration shows Columbus and his men setting up a cross on San Salvador to claim the lands for Spain and the Roman Catholic church. Columbus landed at San Salvador, one of the islands of the Bahamas, on October 12, 1492.

miles long. Not seeing a safe place to land on the eastern side of the island, he ordered his men to sail around it to the western side, where they found a bay and laid anchor. Even before they emerged from the ships, naked natives appeared on the shore, gawking at them. Although the ships were small by European standards, to the natives they seemed large when compared to their small dugout canoes.

Columbus and his men boarded smaller boats and rowed to shore. They carried two banners with them, on which were crowns and the initials F and Y. These initials stood for the king and queen of Spain, Ferdinand and Isabella, who had financed Columbus' voyage. Columbus fell to his knees in the sand, praying and weeping for joy. The banners were planted, and Columbus named the island San Salvador. We now know this island as one of the Bahamas.

Columbus claimed the land for Spain, although there were already people living there. Columbus and other Europeans felt that these people of other lands were savages who needed to be converted to the Christian faith under any circumstances—even by force, if need be. However, Columbus was surprised to discover how friendly the natives were, and remarked that they could "be more easily converted to our Holy Faith through love than by force." He exchanged gifts with them and invited some of them onto his ships. All this had to be done through signs and gestures, as the *interpreter* that Columbus had brought along spoke only Hebrew and Arabic—languages that the explorer had expected people of the Indies to speak.

Columbus wrote down his thoughts in a journal. On the natives, he commented, "They are very well made, with very handsome bodies, and very good countenances. Their hair is short and coarse, almost like the hairs of a horse's tail. They wear the hairs brought down to

Columbus gave the Tainos of Guanahani red caps and glass beads as gifts. In return, the Tainos gave him thread, spears, and pottery.

The Taino people Columbus encountered on his first voyage were the most advanced of the Arawak group of natives living on islands in the Caribbean. The Taino had a sophisticated system of government, as well as their own religion, culture, crafts, and sports. This court where the Taino played ball games dates to before Columbus's arrival.

the eyebrows, except a few locks behind, which they wear long and never cut. They paint themselves black, and they are the color of the Canarians, neither white nor black. . . . They neither carry nor know anything about arms, for I showed them swords, and they took them by the blade and cut themselves through ignorance."

Columbus saw wounds on some of the natives, and they indicated to him that there had been warfare with other peoples from the mainland.

Columbus referred to these people as "Indians," since he thought he was in the West Indies. They had a name, however—the Tainos—and they called their island Guanahani. The Tainos had migrated from South America in their canoes and settled in what are now the Bahamas, Cuba, Jamaica, and Haiti. They constructed their huts out of palm trees. They had a well-maintained agricultural system that yielded corn and potatoes. Though they did not wear clothes, they were skilled at spinning and weaving cotton to make blankets and hammocks. They fired pottery to make their cookware. Columbus took note of these talents, not to praise the Tainos' culture, but to assert that they would make "good servants" for the Europeans.

Columbus noticed that some of the jewelry the natives wore was made out of gold. Of course, there was nothing more important on a mission such as his than finding gold or other valuables. Columbus wanted to be able to bring back boatloads of riches to King Ferdinand and Queen Isabella. Then they would know that the money they had invested in him had been worthwhile.

Columbus asked the natives where they had gotten the gold. When they pointed south, it made perfect sense to him. That was the direction in which Columbus believed Japan was located.

Columbus and his crew stayed on San Salvador for two days. They visited several villages on the island, and each time were greeted warmly and given generous gifts. Natives swam out to the boats with food, fresh water, and even a parrot. Columbus said that parrots were the only animals he saw on the island. All in all, he was quite happy with his discovery. In his diary, he noted that he had found the perfect spot to build a fort: "With 50 men, I could conquer the whole island and govern it as I please." He was not concerned with how the Tainos might feel about that.

On October 14, Columbus and his men set out from Guanahani sailing southward. They had *detained* seven natives on board the *Nina*. Columbus said he needed these men to act as guides to Japan. He also planned to take them back to Spain and "civilize" them. One of the prisoners escaped the next day by jumping overboard. On this same day, Columbus spotted another island, which he

On Christmas Day, 1492, the *Santa Maria* was wrecked when her crew tried to land on a rocky shore. Columbus and his men used the ship's timbers to build a fort. When he sailed back to Spain, 39 crew members were left behind.

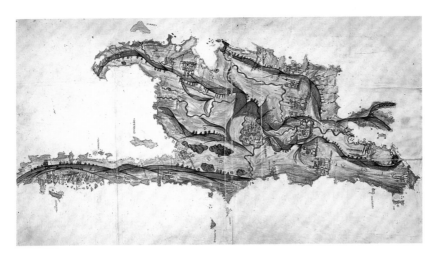

This map of Hispaniola, one of the islands Columbus discovered on his first voyage, was drawn around 1500. The mapmaper may have been Columbus's brother Bartholomew. Several Spanish settlements are indicated by churches, including the capital city of the island, Santo Domingo, which is the second settlement from the right on the southeast coast.

named Santa Maria de la Concepcion. On this island, he again inquired about gold and again was told to go south. The natives did, however, give him a great deal of dried tobacco leaves. Columbus and his men were puzzled as to why the natives seemed to prize this plant, for Europeans had never seen or smoked it before.

For the next few months, Columbus led his ships to several other islands in the area, including Hispaniola (the island that now contains the countries of Haiti and the Dominican Republic) and Cuba. He marveled at the variety of plants and flowers, and called the islands "the best, the most fertile, temperate and beautiful" he had ever seen.

Columbus thought it strange that he saw no mammals whatsoever on his trip, though he saw a gorgeous array of parrots and many reptiles.

After making a final anchorage at a bay that Columbus named Bahia de las Flechas (Bay of the Arrows), where for the first time he encountered unfriendly natives, he decided to head home to Spain. He was eager to report to the king and queen. Columbus and his men **abducted** three more men, seven women, and two boys to bring back to Spain with them.

Although Columbus did not realize it, he had not found a westward passage to the Indies. When he returned to Spain, he was praised and honored for his achievements. However, it would be many years before people would understand the momentous change that would result from his voyage and the exciting new world that he had opened up.

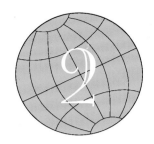

Europe's Quest for Riches

IN THE LATE 1400s, several countries in Western Europe were looking to find new ways to reach the countries of Asia. China, Japan, India, and other countries of the Far East seemed to have an inexhaustible supply of gold, pearls, silk, and *spices*. These luxuries reached Europe by sea, but the process of sailing east around the continent of Africa was dangerous and time-consuming. The rulers of Europe were eager to find quicker, easier passages to the East.

Europeans were also motivated by their religion. England, Spain, Portugal, and Italy were all Christian nations, and their people believed that it was their duty to convert "heathens" to the cross. In the 1490s, Spain finally rid itself of the Moors. These were people from North Africa who followed the religion Islam. They had invaded Spain during the eighth century. After the Moors were finally forced out of Spain in 1492, anti-Muslim feeling was running high. The leaders of the Christian nations were eager to control Muslim expansionism.

Another factor in Europe's renewed interest in exploration was that it had finally emerged from the Dark Ages. Most people living in Europe before the 1200s had been so preoccupied with war and disease that they had little time for learning. By the 15th century, however, a period known as the Renaissance had begun. This was a time when men sought truth in the arts and sciences. Religious myths were being dispelled by education, and new ways of thinking were being encouraged by more open-minded leaders. *Astronomers* and *navigators* attempted to explain the earth's shape and its place in the universe. Average people were beginning to understand such concepts as gravity— why there wasn't really a "top" or "bottom" to the planet they lived on.

For the first time, a merchant class appeared in Europe. These people made their living by trading in the goods that the adventurers brought back from far-off lands. Many of these merchants resided in the city-states of Italy, and those who lived in other Western European countries were forced to go through them in order to buy products from the East. They resented the high prices charged by these traders and put political pressure on their leaders to find ways to bypass the Italian merchants.

For all the cultural and religious factors that contributed to this age of exploration, one practical reason was still the most important: greed. Had there been no potential for profit, the countries of Western Europe would have simply settled into a comfortable ignorance. For the leaders of these countries, the initial investment that had to be made in ships and manpower would not have been worth it had they not been dreaming of the riches that might come back on those ships. And for those daring men who made up the crews of these voyages, the danger and discomfort of the trips would not have been worth it if it were not for the personal fame and wealth they thought they could acquire on their homecoming.

Perhaps no **monarchs** were quite as opportunistic as King Ferdinand and Queen Isabella of Spain. When they married in 1469, the royal Houses of Castile and Aragon were united, and Spain began its rise. Within a decade, it was one of

In 1415, Prince Henry of Portugal was the first to suggest that ships could sail southeast around the continent of Africa in order to reach the Far East.

The region that today is Spain was once divided into several kingdoms. Two of the largest of these states, Aragon and Castile, were united by the 1469 marriage of Ferdinand, the king of Aragon, and Isabella, the queen of Castile. King Ferdinand has been described as an efficient and practical administrator.

the most powerful countries in Europe. Ferdinand and Isabella had no intention of slowing down, however, and wanted to claim for Spain as much land as could be found.

Queen Isabella was an ambitious, intelligent woman. Unlike most women (and even men) in Europe, she was well educated. Her *refinement* and generosity made her popular with the majority of her subjects, but that refinement hid a side that could be ruthless. Isabella did not want any non-Christians in her country. Jews were given the option of converting, but Muslims were driven out forcibly. Ironically, some historians have argued that Columbus, the man who would make Isabella forever famous, came from a Spanish-Jewish family.

At 35 years old, Queen Isabella was the same age as Christopher Columbus when they met for the first time in 1486. A strong-willed, intelligent ruler, Isabella is sometimes called "the Catholic" because of her devotion to the Christian faith.

King Ferdinand did not have his wife's outgoing personality, but he was intelligent and skilled in diplomacy. He and Isabella ruled their colonies with an iron fist.

With their land at peace and more money than they knew what to do with, Ferdinand and Isabella might have seemed like easy targets for a young adventurer in need of financial backing. But the road to exploration would prove to be a long and winding one.

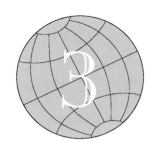

The Life and Travels of Columbus

THE MAN WE call Christopher Columbus was probably born in 1451, the same year as Queen Isabella, in Genoa, Italy. His father, Domenico, was a weaver who also owned a tavern and dabbled in real estate. He married Columbus' mother, Susanna Fontana-Rossa, in the late 1440s. Susanna gave birth to four boys and a girl. Christopher was their eldest son.

Genoa was a bustling port city, and Columbus was exposed to sailing at an early age. In a letter to King Ferdinand and Queen Isabella in 1501, he says, "At a very tender age I became a sailor, and I have continued until this day . . . For 40 years I have followed this trade." That would

This painting of the busy harbor at Genoa was made in 1481. The important port city in Italy probably looked like this 30 years earlier, when Christopher Columbus was born.

have made Columbus about 10 years old when his sailing career began. It is likely that he was exaggerating to impress his *patrons*, for Columbus told his son, Ferdinand, that his first sea voyage was at the age of 14. At any rate, there is no doubt that he was quite young when he started his life as a sailor.

Columbus was willing to work for whoever would pay him well. In 1476 he hired to work on a Portuguese ship. The vessel he served on attacked his home town, Genoa. When the ship he was working on caught fire that same year, Columbus jumped overboard and swam several miles to the shore of Portugal while clinging to a wooden oar.

Christopher Columbus is an English version of the explorer's name. He was born Cristoforo Colombo. The Spanish called him Cristobal Colon.

The capitol of Portugal, Lisbon, was a thriving center of trade and home to many colorful seafaring characters. Columbus must have grown up fast among these worldly and exciting men. He also gained an informal education from the many scientists and astronomers who lived in Lisbon, who often spoke of reaching the Far East by sailing west. An astronomer from Florence, Paolo Toscanelli, took Columbus under his wing, teaching him scientific principles and encouraging his dreams of exploration.

In the late 1470s and early 1480s, Columbus made many merchant voyages to faraway places. He sailed north to Iceland and south to Guinea, on the coast of Africa.

In 1478, Columbus married Filipa Perestrello y Moniz, the daughter of a sea captain whose family was one of the most powerful in Spain. Soon after, their son, Diego, was

When Christopher Columbus was four years old, the German Johann Guttenburg invented the printing press. The first book ever printed was a 42-line Bible.

born. Their happiness was short-lived, however, as Filipa died in 1483. It is not known how hard Columbus took her death, as he never mentions her in any of his writings. Although his wife was gone, the connections he had made during their marriage would prove to be invaluable to him.

Columbus was now consumed with the idea of a westward voyage to find the West Indies, and he was willing to take funding from any government that would offer it. Over the next nine years, he would repeatedly approach four monarchs: King John II of Portugal, King Henry VII of England, and Ferdinand and Isabella of Spain. Year after year, he was turned away or put off, but Columbus refused to give up. Finally, in 1492, he was granted a royal passport by Spain and given the use of three small boats: the *Nina*, the *Pinta*, and the *Santa Maria*. The biggest of these, the *Santa Maria*, was only about 90 feet long.

> **Columbus wrote a book on Biblical prophecy, which he sent to King Ferdinand and Queen Isabella. He was trying to get them to authorize a crusade to the Holy Lands, but the monarchs decided against it.**

Columbus's first order of business was to decide who would accompany him on his voyage. Luis de Torres was chosen specifically because he could speak Hebrew and Arabic, and might be used as an interpreter. Martín Alonso

Columbus says farewell to two of his friends, Antonio Marchena and Juan Pérez, as he prepares to depart from Palos, a Spanish port near the border of Portugal. Marchena and Pérez were monks living at the nearby monastery La Rabida. Columbus himself stayed at the monastery while waiting for King Ferdinand and Queen Isabella to decide whether to support his proposed expedition. Columbus left Palos on August 3, 1492.

Pinzón, a highly regarded sea captain, would command the *Pinta*, and his brother, Vincente Yáñez Pinzón, would take charge of the *Nina*. Three doctors were hired, one for each ship. Strangely, when one considers what devout Christians Ferdinand and Isabella were, it is odd that no clergymen accompanied the crew. This may be a clue that the voyage was far more important to Columbus himself than to his patrons. The king and queen may have simply been worn down by Columbus' repeated pleadings and gave in to make him go away. The amount of money they gave Columbus was very small when compared with what they had.

Columbus and his men set sail on August 2, 1492. After two months at sea, Columbus spotted land. He soon claimed many islands—including the Bahamas, Cuba, Hispaniola, and Jamaica—for Spain.

Not all was smooth sailing on this expedition, however. There was friction almost right from the start between Columbus and Martin Pinzón. Pinzón was a strong, confident man who was used to leading his own voyages—not taking orders from others. As Columbus was sailing from island to island, Pinzón became restless. On November 21, 1492, he and the crew of the *Pinta* committed **mutiny**. They left Columbus's other two ships and went looking for gold on their own.

Columbus was disgusted, but not surprised. He reported

in his journal that Pinzón had already "caused many other troubles by word and deed." He may have actually been rather relieved to be rid of him. Pinzón went off and found the island of Babeque, but he did not find any gold there.

Several months later, the *Pinta* rejoined the main group. Pinzón made up a flimsy excuse about being forced by crewmen to lead his own expedition. Columbus knew his story wasn't true and wanted to turn him away, but he was afraid to do so. Many men, not only on the *Pinta* but also on the two other ships, preferred Pinzón's leadership style to Columbus's. The explorer would just have to put up with Pinzón until they returned home.

The *Santa Maria* was left behind after it was shipwrecked, and the men started for Spain in the *Pinta* and the *Nina*. On the homeward journey, Columbus's two ships were separated again—this time by a terrible storm. The *Pinta* arrived in Spain first, while the *Nina* was forced to land in Portugal. Martin Pinzón went to the palace to tell King Ferdinand and Queen Isabella of the journey. They declined to see him, however, saying that they preferred to wait for Columbus.

Pinzón's hatred for Columbus was now total. He refused to report to him at landing and was even too depressed to say hello to his own brother, Vincente, when the *Nina* docked at Palos. He had become sick during the long voyage, and died soon after he arrived in Spain.

Columbus received a great deal of glory and *adulation* from his first journey, but he was not one to rest on his laurels. He immediately began planning his second trip to the New World, again hoping to reach the Far East. Ferdinand and Isabella had learned that King John of Portugal was planning a westward voyage, and they were worried about the land he might claim. They therefore helped Columbus in every way they could, placing him in charge of a fleet of 17 ships.

Columbus had no trouble finding a crew this time, for his fame had spread, and it seemed that every sailor in Spain wanted to be a part of his next adventure. Military officers, physicians, priests, journalists, and even the mayor of the town of Baeza were on board. When the fleet departed from Cadíz on September 25, 1493, about 1,200 men accompanied Columbus.

One member of Columbus's second expedition was a soldier named Juan Ponce de León. He would later gain fame by landing on Puerto Rico and in Florida.

Columbus sailed first to the Canary Islands, where food and supplies for the proposed new settlement were picked up. From there, they sailed southwest, and after three weeks, land was sighted. It was an island that Columbus

Columbus's coat-of-arms, created during the excitement of his return to Spain in 1493, features symbols of King Ferdinand and Queen Isabella (a castle, representing Castille, and a lion, representing Aragon). The islands and anchors are personal elements for the admiral of the western sea, as Columbus was called.

named Dominica. Four other islands were sighted in quick succession. On one of them, Guadaloupe, Columbus and his men had a frightening encounter with *cannibals*, but the cannibals were afraid of the Spaniards and ran away, leaving the evidence of their gruesome eating habits behind. This was not enough to make the Spaniards lose their appetites, however, and they were thrilled to discover a new fruit on this island: the pineapple.

Many other islands were discovered on this second voyage, including Antigua, St. Croix, and the Virgin Islands. Eventually, Hispaniola was reached. Columbus and his men were saddened to learn that the men they had left behind on the first trip had been *massacred* by the natives. The whole colony was gone. On Hispaniola,

Columbus and his men founded a new town, Isabella, and began building huts and planting crops. Relations between the settlers went downhill fast, however. They argued over supplies and food and how much work needed to be done. Then, about 400 of the men, including Columbus, contracted *malaria*. Over the next several years, complaints

Disgraced, Christopher Columbus sits in the hold of a ship that is returning to Spain. Although Columbus was a brave explorer and an accomplished sailor, he was not a very good governor of Spain's colonies in the lands he had claimed for Spain. Eventually, Columbus was replaced as governor and ordered to return to Spain; the new governor humiliated Columbus by insisting that he be arrested and handcuffed. The king and queen ordered the chains to be removed, but Columbus remained bitter about the experience for the rest of his life.

about Columbus got back to Ferdinand and Isabella in Spain. He was finally forced in 1496 to return to Spain and defend himself against attacks by his enemies at court.

On his third voyage to the New World, from 1498 to 1500, Columbus' heavy-handed leadership finally brought him down. After discovering the South American mainland, Columbus became embroiled in a feud with the royal governor, who supported those men who had revolted against him. The governor felt that he had no choice but to arrest Columbus and send him back to Spain in irons. The king and queen did not approve of what the governor had done, but they felt that Columbus should retire. Against their wishes, in 1502, Columbus made one last voyage, in which he explored the coast of Central America.

In his last years, Columbus was bitter and lonely. He died on May 20, 1506, at the age of 55, without ever realizing—or being able to admit—that he had placed the continents of North and South America on European maps.

Snor

posto que os capitaães moor desta v'ra fora e asi os
outros capitaães ãouam a vossa alteza auora de aqui
meus dsta v'ra ... nova epr' ã ora nosso ... ...
quem achou. nom teporees tam bem de ... ...
... ...ta a vossa alteza ate ... ou mjlhor
pode a ... pas bras rontar e falar ... ...
... que todos ... p' tome vossa alteza ...
... ... bras ... ...
... ... de p'ie ...
... ... pasões e danla ...
... ... Darey ... ...
... vossa alteza ... ... nom ... ...
... ... Snor
... ... falar ... ...
... ... vossa alteza ... foy ...
... ... sabado ... do dito mes ...
... ... outras ... ... as ...
... pera dagram ... ...
... dia ... ... ou
... legoas. ... domjngo ... do dito mes a...
... ... mais ou ... ...
... ...
... pilote. ... ...
... ... pedro da costa v'este ... ...
... ...
... pode ... ... os capitaães ... ...
... a... ... outros pares ... ...
... ...
... terca feira ... ... que bram ...
... ... que topamos ... ...
... ou ... ...
... ... romp... ... ...
... ... outros ... ...
... ... cada quarta feira ... ...

A letter from Pedro Álvares Cabral, a Portuguese sailor who followed Vasco da Gama's route to India. During his voyage, Cabral spotted the Brazilian coast of South America. This letter tells what Cabral found when he explored Brazil in 1500.

The Rivals of Columbus

COLUMBUS IS THE MOST famous of all Renaissance navigators, but other men of the sea were leaving their mark on history during the same time as well. Many of them were sponsored by the king of Portugal, Manuel I, who had been crowned when King John II died in 1495. Manuel presided over the last years of what is considered to be the golden age of Portuguese discovery. His interest in the arts and sciences was reflected in his court, and although he was a very religious man, he was also open to new ideas. This combination of missionary zeal and curiosity led him to help a number of young explorers, among them Amerigo Vespucci, Pedro Álvarez Cabral, and the Corte-Real brothers.

Amerigo Vespucci was born in Florence, Italy, on March 9, 1451. His father, Nastagio, was a **notary**. Little is known of his mother, aside from the fact that her name was Lisabetta. His uncle, Giorgio Antonio, was a teacher to the noble families of Florence. Giorgio taught his nephew about philosophy, literature, and Latin. It is possible that Vespucci also studied under Toscanelli, the teacher of Columbus. As he grew, Vespucci's interests turned to physics, geometry, and astronomy.

In 1478, another relative, Guido Antonio Vespucci, took the young Amerigo with him to Paris when he was appointed Italy's ambassador to France. Here, Vespucci made many important friends, including Duke Rene of Lorraine, and completed his education. He then went to Seville, Spain, where he worked as a financial advisor to one of the banking houses of the Medicis, a powerful Italian family. The Medicis had just begun sponsoring oceanic expeditions, and Vespucci eagerly learned all he could about navigation.

Vespucci's first voyage was sponsored by King Ferdinand of Spain, who gave him the use of three ships, just as he had granted to Columbus on his first expedition. Vespucci set sail west from Cadíz on May 10, 1497. After several weeks, the mainland of North America was spotted. His ships explored the Gulf of Mexico and the southern coastline of

Amerigo Vespucci explored the coast of South America for both Spain and Portugal. Unlike Columbus, Vespucci understood that North and South America were continents that had previously been unknown to Europeans. Vespucci also wrote many letters about the places he visited and the people he met during his expeditions. In 1507, German mapmaker Martin Waldseemüller applied Vespucci's first name to the new continent: America.

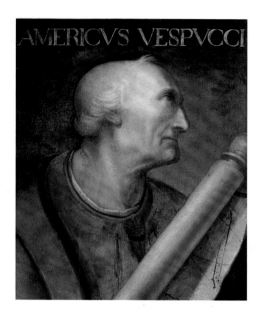

what is now the United States. He returned to Spain in October 1498.

On his second voyage, Vespucci went farther south, crossing the equator and exploring the length of Brazil. He discovered Cape St. Augustine and the Amazon River. When he returned to Spain in 1500, he was very ill. He spent several months *recuperating* and wrote long letters about the voyage to his friends Duke Rene of Lorraine and Lorenzo de Medici.

Vespucci's next three voyages were sponsored by King Manuel I of Portugal. All of these were expeditions of South America, during which Vespucci and his men found an abundance of gold and pearls, which they brought back to Portugal. Although Vespucci sailed for Portugal between

1501 and 1505 and claimed many areas of South America for King Manuel I, this in no way tarnished his reputation in Spain. King Ferdinand and his people were grateful to him, and he felt comfortable making a home there when his career was over. He eventually became a Spanish citizen and died in Seville on February 22, 1512.

Pedro Álvarez Cabral was a Portuguese navigator who sailed under the flag of Portugal at around the same time as Vespucci. He must have been well connected at court, for King Manuel chose him to carry on the exploration begun by Vasco da Gama, who had made the first successful sea voyage to India in 1497–99. Gama personally wrote a set of directions for Cabral, and in 1500, King Manuel placed Cabral in command of a fleet of 13 ships. The king com-

Pedro Álvarez Cabral was born around 1460 to Fernao Cabral, the governor of Beria and Belmonte, and his wife, Isabel de Gouvea. Little is known of Cabral's early years, but that fact that he came from a prominent family means that he was probably well educated.

King Manuel I of Portugal

Manuel I, king of Portugal from 1495 to 1521, was only 21 years old when he took the throne. Manuel was born in 1469, and took the throne after the death of his uncle, King John II. King Manuel continued King John's program of exploration. Although the voyages of Vasco da Gama and other Portuguese explorers had been planned under King John, the expeditions began under Manuel I.

The success of explorers like Gama and Cabral brought vast wealth to Portugal, but with this wealth came problems. It corrupted officials and turned focus away from other Portuguese industries. In addition, Manuel I suffered pressures from Spain to expel Jews from his country. But the king used the wealth for positive endeavors, erecting buildings throughout his newly expanded kingdom.

Manuel will be remembered most for his contribution to the age of exploration. In fact, history has dubbed him "Manuel the Fortunate" because he inherited this great program. He died in 1521.

missioned him to explore India and also ordered Cabral to open up permanent trade routes with India and spread Christianity to the people of the Far East.

The fleet set sail from Lisbon on March 9, 1500, with a crew of 1,000 aboard. Cabral and his men were supposed to sail along the Cape of Good Hope route that Vasco da

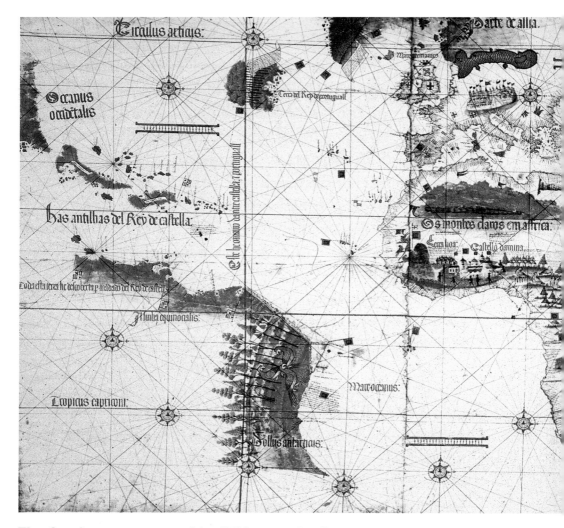

The Cantino map, created in 1502, was the first map to show Brazil, discovered by Pedro Álvarez Cabral two years earlier. The vertical blue line through Brazil shows a boundary established by Pope Alexander VI in 1494; under the Treaty of Tordesillas, Portugal would have rights to new lands and routes of discovery to the

Gama had pioneered. They would follow the coast of Africa south, then sail southwest into the Atlantic Ocean, then swing back to the southeast and pass the southernmost tip

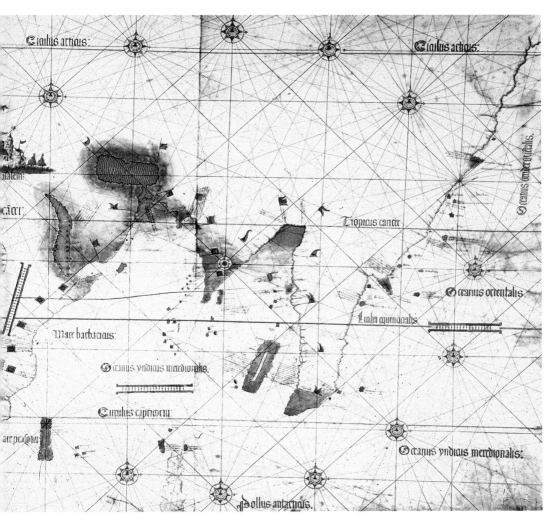

east, while Spain would control the lands to the west, including North America and most of South America. Portuguese possessions are marked with red and blue flags, while Spanish discoveries, including the islands visited by Columbus, are marked with the banner of Ferdinand and Isabella.

of Africa. By swinging in an arc away from the African coast, the ships would avoid dangerous currents. However, Cabral's fleet was caught in a storm, which drove them farther west than Gama had gone. On April 22, the fleet reached a harbor called Porto Seguro in what is now Brazil. Cabral claimed the territory for Portugal, and sent a ship back to tell King Manuel what had happened.

When the weather improved, Cabral sailed eastward, intending to complete the voyage. Then disaster struck: Four of his vessels were destroyed in a storm off the Cape of Good Hope, and many crew members died. Cabral pushed on, however, and he and the rest of the fleet reached Calicut, India, on September 13. Once there, he successfully negotiated a commercial *treaty* with the town's leader and set up a permanent trading post. Cabral returned to Portugal on July 31, 1501. Nothing is known of his later life, but he is believed to have died in 1526.

Perhaps the most mysterious of the explorers of this time were the Corte-Real brothers, Vasco, Miguel, and Gaspar. Their father, Jõao, was the cruel, iron-fisted ruler of several islands in the Azores. He had kidnapped a woman from there and forced her to marry him. Little is known of the childhood years of their three sons, but it is believed that Gaspar, the youngest, was born in 1450. When Jõao died in 1496, Vasco inherited his islands, but never once even visited them. He lived in Portugal, but did send his two younger brothers to be raised in the Azores.

There was much to learn about navigation in the

Azores, and Miguel and Gaspar were skilled sailors by the time they were young men. Gaspar served Manuel before his ascension to the throne of Portugal and was a member of his court after he became king. In May 1500, King Manuel granted Gaspar the property and trading rights to any lands he might discover. The Corte-Reals' immense wealth is reflected in the fact that Gaspar paid for his own voyages—he did not have to wait around for the permission of a monarch. There is no doubt that as a rich man, Gaspar was able to pick the very best ships he could find.

That summer, Gaspar set out on his expedition. Few records exist that document

The property rights to Newfoundland remained in the Corte-Real family until 1578, when the last male heir, Manuel Corte-Real, died in battle fighting the Moors.

this voyage, but it is known that several weeks later, the party reached North America. The land was so green and fertile and with such large trees, that Gaspar named it Terre Verte, or Greenland. He also explored the areas now known as Labrador and Newfoundland. He returned to Lisbon in the fall of 1500.

On his second voyage to Newfoundland in 1501, Gaspar and his men kidnapped 57 Native Americans and brought them back to Portugal. These were people of the Beothuk tribe, and we can only imagine their sorrow at

The Beothuk tribe, who were discovered by Gaspar's expedition party, was driven into the interior of North America by French and English settlers. The tribe was eventually exterminated.

being taken from their families to be enslaved in a strange land. Relatively few Native Americans were taken to Europe to become slaves, unlike Africans, who were captured in huge numbers. Most North and South American explorers kidnapped natives simply to show their sponsors what the people of the New World looked like, but for the victims, it was a heartbreaking and terrifying experience.

The two ships containing the slaves reached Lisbon between October 9 and 11, 1501. The third ship, which carried Gaspar, was lost and never heard from again. Gaspar's brother, Miguel, embarked on a rescue mission in January 1502. His ship was also lost. In the spring of 1503, the last remaining Corte-Real brother, Vasco, went looking for both his siblings. He survived his voyage, but found no trace of either Gaspar or Miguel.

In the story of America's rediscovery by Europeans, the adventures of the Corte-Real brothers are often overlooked. Part of the reason for this was the secrecy under which their voyages were conducted. Portuguese voyages were usually planned and carried out in secrecy, and this one was no exception. Few letters or other documents related to the voyage have survived. Also, King Manuel did not want to offend England, a country with which Portugal had friendly relations. The Corte-Reals were sailing to lands that had been claimed by the English king a few years earlier, after the voyage of a remarkable explorer, John Cabot.

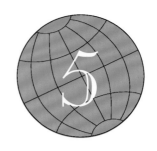

John Cabot's Voyages for England

IN 1497, AN ITALIAN sailor named John Cabot returned to England after sailing west across the Atlantic. Cabot said he had found new lands far to the north of Columbus's New World discoveries. The landing of Cabot at Newfoundland would eventually help England take its place as one of the world's greatest seafaring powers.

We know Cabot today by the English version of his name, but when he was born around 1451 in Italy, his name was Giovanni Caboto. The name Caboto means "coaster"—one who lives on the coast and is involved in some type of shipping. Cabot's father was an Italian merchant. Cabot was born in an Italian city, either Gaeta or Genoa.

Cabot moved to Venice in 1461 and became a Venetian citizen in 1476. In 1482, he married a woman named Mattea, and they had three sons: Ludovico, Sebastiano, and Sancio. Cabot bought and sold real estate and traded in Asian spices and silks. Cabot's interest in navigation grew as he heard stories of the great adventurers of his time, and he longed to explore the Atlantic as they had.

Cabot moved his young family to Velencia, a port city in Spain, in 1490. Through his business dealings, he had learned that Italian merchants had a *monopoly* on the spice-trading business. Cabot reasoned that the Spanish and Portugese rulers would want to find a new way to reach Asia, a way that would avoid the Mediterranean, and, therefore, the Italians. He first approached King Ferdinand of Spain in 1493, but the king was not willing to put up all the money, and Cabot could not find other investors.

Soon, Cabot heard about the successful first voyage of Columbus. Like all other Europeans, he must have thought that Columbus had reached some islands off the coast of Southeast Asia, but had not quite made it to the mainland. He approached Spain again, and then Portugal, but neither was interested. The monarchs of both countries felt satisfied with the explorations they were already funding.

Cabot turned to England in 1495, knowing that King Henry VII bitterly regretted having turned down the

King Henry VII of England agreed to support Cabot's voyage. The king hoped to claim lands in the New World that would contain a route to the Far East. This would help keep England on a par with the other nations which were actively searching for a way to the Indies.

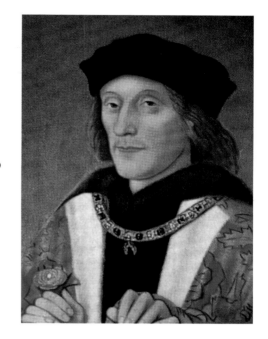

chance to sponsor Columbus's first voyage. Cabot apparently had more money now than when he had approached Spain a few years before, or maybe he was willing to settle for less, because he didn't ask the king for any funding, only that he be allowed to travel under the protection of the British crown. Henry VII eagerly agreed. He granted Cabot the right to explore the "countryes, regions or provinces of the heathen and infedelles . . . which before this time have been unknown to all Christians."

Cabot settled in the English port city of Bristol and set about planning his voyage. One of his friends and financial backers was the sheriff of Bristol, Richard Amerike. Bristol was a small city of only about 10,000 people, but it was a very

Some people believe that America was named for Cabot's friend in Bristol, Richard Amerike.

wealthy place, thanks to the shipping business. Many merchants in Bristol were counting on Cabot to make them even wealthier. Since the voyage was a private venture, Cabot was able to obtain only one ship, the *Matthew*. It was a small vessel, about the same size as Columbus' *Nina*, and could hold 50 tons of cargo.

The exploration party of 20 men set sail from Bristol on May 20, 1497. Most of the men were Bristol natives, but the doctor was from Genoa, and Cabot's sons may also have been along. Cabot sailed down the Bristol Channel, out to Ireland, and north up the western Irish coast before heading west into the Atlantic.

After 35 days, North America was sighted. Historians, however, are still debating where in North America Cabot landed. No original maps or logbooks have survived from the voyage, but many scholars believe that Cabot landed in the area called Newfoundland, on Cape Bonavista. Cabot and his men explored the coast for several months, then sped back across the ocean to England in just 15 days.

Some historians believe that Cabot landed on North America within about five miles of the spot where Leif Eriksson, the Norwegian explorer, had tried to found a settlement in 1001.

King Henry VII was ecstatic. Cabot had not found any riches, but then neither had Columbus. England was back in the race for new lands, and Henry wanted Cabot to sail again as soon as possible.

In Cabot's time, most ships were named after Christian saints. Matthew was the author of one of the gospels. However, Cabot may also have named his ship after his wife, Mattea.

Having proved himself on the first crossing, Cabot was rewarded by the king, who gave the explorer a small grant of money. Henry VII also gave Cabot five ships to use for his second voyage. In May 1498, the fleet sailed from Bristol. One ship was damaged in a storm and returned to port soon after. It is thought that the others went the same route as during the first voyage and further explored the coast of North America.

What is known for sure is that John Cabot died on this voyage. He may have been shipwrecked and starved to death. He may have been killed by Beothuk natives. Regardless of what happened, he never returned to England. Cabot's son, Sebastiano (or Sebastian), carried on his father's work, serving as a navigator under the kings of both Spain and England.

The explorers of the 15th and 16th centuries were not the first Europeans to "discover" North and South America. The Vikings had visited the coast of North America nearly 500 years earlier. However, unlike the Viking visits, the voyages of Columbus, Cabot, and others would forever change the future of the New World.

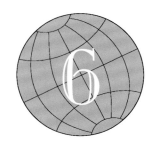

A New Beginning, A Tragic End

IN RECENT YEARS, there has been a great debate in our country as to how Americans today should view the European explorers of the New World. Some people feel that Columbus's voyages should be celebrated with a holiday and parades; others maintain that these celebrations are insensitive to the sufferings of Native American people. Some argue over whether it was Amerigo Vespucci or Richard Amerike who lent his name to the continent we live on; others say that it should not be named after any European.

Probably the worst thing that could be done would be to oversimplify the issues. Columbus, Vespucci, Cabot, and the rest were living in complicated times. Though they called themselves Christians, they were still only human and made many mistakes. At times, their ambition and greed blinded them to the cruelties they were inflicting on a race of people they considered inferior. The Europeans obviously believed the Tainos and other Native Americans to be fully human; if they had not believed them to have souls, they would not have bothered trying to convert them to Christianity. On the other hand, it is clear from the documentation left behind that rather than live side-by-side with native peoples, Europeans intended from the very first to conquer them and destroy their cultures.

This is not to say that all Native Americans were peace-loving innocents. Warfare and slavery among the native peoples existed long before the Europeans came. Columbus and his men even found evidence of cannibalism on one island. Just as some Europeans were greedy, some natives were greedy as well. In exchange for money or items they thought were valuable, they were willing to aid in the downfall of other native tribes.

Although it took several centuries for white Europeans to make serious inroads into Native American territory, their effect was felt long before their actual presence. The early explorers and colonists brought with them diseases that the natives' immune systems were not equipped to fight off. Tribes living on or near the east coast of North America were the hardest hit, but the viruses quickly spread inland as the natives moved west, away from the white settlements.

Of course, the spread of disease was not something that the Europeans did consciously or maliciously. The Europeans simply did not understand the way viruses worked any more than the Native Americans did. They did not even know that the washing of hands could prevent the spread of disease. The Europeans of the time were not very aware of good hygene. The ships that they sailed to the New World in were often filthy and rat-infested. These rats ran ashore and reproduced, posing a terrible health threat to all humans in the area.

In most cases, the early explorers found the Native American peoples to be friendly and generous. Columbus frankly stated how surprised he had been to make friends with the Tainos. As the years went on, however, the natives began to realize that the Europeans had much more in mind than a settlement or two. They began to understand that their whole way of life was under siege. By the time the truth dawned on them, however, it was probably already too late. Their bows and arrows were no match for the Europeans' firearms, and their bodies could not stand up to foreign diseases.

Well-armed Spanish soldiers fight Aztec warriors in Spain during the 1520s. The Aztecs may have had the most powerful military in the New World, yet a few hundred Spanish conquistadors, led by Hernán Cortés, managed to conquer them within a few years. Horses, metal armor, sharp swords, and an early type of firearm called an arquebus contributed to the Europeans' military success in North and South America.

For Europeans, of course, the opening up of the New World was a far more positive experience. Men such as Columbus and Cabot were glorified as heroes who had brought national honor to their countries. After the horror of the Dark Ages, people finally had reason to feel good again and to look to the future with optimism. Instead of living in fear and superstition, average citizens had faith that a new era of reason and tolerant Christianity was upon them. And if the monarchs they lived under became tyrannical, the New World offered the hope of a new beginning.

Make no mistake, though, that life for the average person in the late 1400s and early 1500s was very, very hard—whether they lived in Europe or North America. We cannot imagine in our technologically advanced world just how brutal day-to-day life was in those times. The average man was lucky to live past his 40th birthday. Mothers often lost their lives in childbirth, and it was quite common for children and babies to die.

This is not to excuse the crimes that were committed in the opening of the New World. The European explorers were often cruel and exploitative in their adventures. There is no doubt that the harsh realities of life in their times contributed to the **bigotry** and ignorance they sometimes displayed in their travels. Rather than judge them on the standards of the 21st century, however, we would be wise to learn from their mistakes and to resolve not to repeat them.

Chronology

1415 Prince Henry of Portugal is the first European to suggest that ships could sail southeast around Africa to reach the Indies.

1450 Gaspar Corte-Real is born.

1451 Christopher Columbus, Amerigo Vespucci, John Cabot, and Queen Isabella of Spain are born.

1460 Pedro Álvarez Cabral is born.

1476 Columbus is hired by the Portuguese ship; when the ship sinks he is forced to swim several miles to the coast of Portugal.

1469 Ferdinand of Castile and Isabella of Aragon are married, uniting two kingdoms into what will become the modern nation of Spain.

1481 King John II takes the throne in Portugal and pushes an ambitious program of exploration forward.

1492 Columbus sails west across the Atlantic Ocean, expecting to find China; instead, he finds a number of islands off the coast of America.

1494 Columbus makes his second voyage to the New World.

1496 John Cabot sets out from England, intending to sail west across the Atlantic, but is forced to turn back.

1497 Cabot again sets out from England, this time landing on Newfoundland and claiming the area for England;

Amerigo Vespucci makes his first voyage in the service of Spain.

1498 Columbus makes his third voyage, during which he lands on the coast of South America; John Cabot is lost at sea while returning to Newfoundland.

1500 Pedro Álvarez Cabral sets sail from Lisbon for India, and accidentally lands in Brazil, which he claims for Spain. Gaspar Corte-Real makes his first voyage to North America.

1501 Gaspar Corte-Real is lost at sea; Amerigo Vespucci begins sailing under the Portuguese flag.

1502 Miguel Corte-real is lost at sea while searching for his brother, Gaspar.

1507 The name "America" is applied to the continents in the Atlantic Ocean for the first time by German mapmaker Martin Waldseemüller.

Glossary

Abduct—to carry off a person by force; kidnap.

Adulation—extreme flattery or admiration.

Astronomer—someone who specializes in studying the stars, planets, and other celestial bodies.

Bigotry—the state of being extremely devoted to one's opinions or prejudices and a refusal to listen to other ideas.

Cannibal—somebody who eats human flesh.

Detain—to hold or keep as if in custody.

Interpreter—someone who translates orally what is said in one language into another language, so that people who speak different languages can communicate.

Malaria—a disease transmitted by mosquitoes and characterized by chills and fever.

Massacre—the vicious killing of a large number of people.

Monarch—a person who reigns over a kingdom or empire.

Monopoly—exclusive possession or control, usually of a particular good or service.

Mutiny—a revolt (as of a naval crew) against authority or a superior officer.

Glossary

Navigator—a person who is skilled at plotting and following a course from one place to another, and of determining the position of a ship or other vehicle.

Notary—a public officer who certifies writings and makes them authentic.

Patron—a person who uses wealth and influence to help another.

Recuperate—to recover from an illness or injury.

Refinement—the state of being cultured.

Spices—aromatic vegetable products used to season or flavor foods. These were very valuable in Europe during the 15th and 16th centuries because they were not easily available.

Treaty—a document in which an agreement between two or more parties is written down.

Further Reading

Dor-Ner, Zvi. *Columbus and the Age of Discovery.* New York: William Morrow, 1991.

Gallagher, Jim. *The Viking Explorers.* Philadelphia: Chelsea House, 2001.

Konstam, Angus. *Historical Atlas of Exploration, 1492–1600.* New York: Checkmark Books, 2000.

Rientis, Rex, and Thea Rientis. *The Voyages of Columbus.* New York: Crescent Books, 1989.

Rutsala, David. *The Sea Route to Asia.* Philadelphia: Mason Crest Publishers, 2003.

Shields, Charles J. *John Cabot and the Rediscovery of North America.* Philadelphia: Chelsea House Publishers, 2002.

Internet Resources

Christopher Columbus

http://www.nmm.ac.uk?education/fact_columbus.html

http://www.acs.ucalgary.ca/HIST/tutor/eurovoya/columbus.html

http://geonames.nrcan.gc.ca/english/schoolnet/nfld/johncobo.html

John Cabot

http://www.heritage.nf.ca/exploration/cabot.html

http://www.newadvent.org/cathen?12104a.htm

Pedro Álvarez Cabral

http://www.newadvent.org/cathen/15384.htm

http://www.newadvent.org/cathen/03128a.htm

http://www.millenium-exhibit.org/milanich1.htm

Index

Photo Credits

About the Author

Kelly Wittmann has written a novel, as well as dozens of articles on history, art, and literature. She lives in Milwaukee, Wisconsin.